Buses, Coaches, Trams Recollections 1971

Contents

Introduction   3

Scotland   3
Teesside   6
Isle of Man   6
Lancashire and Merseyside   7
Yorkshire   17
Staffordshire   23
Derbyshire   24
Nottingham and Leicester   26
Walsall and Birmingham   31
East Midlands   34
Oxford, Cheltenham and Bristol   36
Wales   42
London   42
South Coast   44
The South West   46

1971 No 1 Records   16
1971 Happenings   32, 35, 41, 45, 47
1971 Arrivals & Departures   47

Index of operators and Vehicles   48

Acknowledgments

A large number of the illustrations in this book are from the camera of Bob Gell, and without them and the detailed notes on each slide this book would not have been possible. My most sincere thanks to Bob – outstanding! Many thanks also to the Omnibus Society for their kind permission to access the collection of Peter Taplin, which is very much appreciated.

The PSV Circle Fleet Histories for the operators in this book and a number of issues of *Buses Illustrated* were vital sources of information.

British Library Cataloguing in Publication Data

A catalogue record for this book is available from the British Library.

ISBN 978 1 85794 460 0

Silver Link Publishing Ltd
The Trundle
Ringstead Road
Great Addington
Kettering
Northants NN14 4BW

Tel/Fax: 01536 330588
email: sales@nostalgiacollection.com
Website: www.nostalgiacollection.com

Printed and bound in the Czech Republic

Title page: **SHEFFIELD** Working the Walkley-City-Intake service 95 on 15 August 1971 is No 1273 (VWE 73), a Roe-bodied AEC Regent III new in 1955. *Author's collection*

About the author

My first recollections of public transport were early in 1958 in my home town of Aberdeen, travelling from our home in Mastrick to Union Street, then onwards by tram to Bridge of Dee. My interest in buses, trolleybuses and trams expanded to taking fleet numbers or registration numbers, and by the mid-1960s I had acquired a camera and began my collection. This interest continued through my family's moves from Aberdeen to Perth, Whitburn in West Lothian, Banbury, Swindon and Oxford by 1974.

My first job was with Customs & Excise, beginning in London with transfers to Oxford, Dover and Brighton. It was after I left Brighton that my enthusiasm for bus photography waned, and it never really returned apart from sporadic photography when I returned to Scotland in 1980. By this time I had left Customs & Excise and had returned to college in Cupar to study Agriculture. I met my future wife at this college and moved with her parents to Galloway, where I have lived very happily since 1983. To further my career I attended Aberdeen University to take a BSc Degree in Agriculture, and I successfully graduated in 1996. This led to me returning to the Civil Service with the Scottish Executive Rural Affairs Department, then through many changes to where I am now, working with Natural England as adviser to farmers on Environmental Schemes (three days a week from last July).

By 2010 I had a significant collection of transport views from the mid-1960s to the early 1980s. I met with Silver Link Publishing's editor Will Adams in Preston in early 2010 and was very kindly given the opportunity to write a volume on Buses, Trams and Trolleybuses in the Midlands. Since then I have continued to enjoy writing volumes on transport for Silver Link, this volume being my fifth in the 'Recollections' series looking at buses, trolleybuses and trams as well as significant events in a specific year.

Introduction

In 1971 the miniskirt was still in fashion, Edward Heath was resident at No 10, and the Divorce Reform Act made it much easier for a couple to escape a marriage; apart from variations in Scotland, the Act still forms the basis of Britain's divorce law today. The Act created the so-called 'quickie divorce' and introduced the principle of 'irretrievable breakdown' as grounds for separation.

This year Britain adopted decimal currency and 20 shillings to £1 was substituted by 100 new pence. The new coins – ½p, 1p, 2p, 5p, 10p, 50p – swiftly replaced the old pounds, shillings and pence. There was concern about public rejection, fears that bus crews would refuse to handle the new coinage, and Ford car workers threatened to strike over alterations to drink vending machine prices. However, the transition went relatively smoothly.

Television audience ratings figures revealed that *The Benny Hill Show* was the most-watched light entertainment show on ITV. The entertainer also hit the No 1 spot in the charts with *Ernie (The Fastest Milkman in the West)*.

Overseas, in Uganda Idi Amin, a former British colonial army sergeant and heavyweight boxer, seized power from Milton Obote and established dictatorial control. America's most-wanted serial killer, Charles Manson, was finally brought to justice for the murder of actress Sharon Tate, the wife of Roman Polanski, their unborn son and Steve Parent, Abigail Folger, Voytek Frykowski and Jay Sebring at Polanski's rented Beverley Hills home. On 15 January 1971, seven months after the trial began, the jury took just nine days to find Manson and four of his followers guilty of murder and they were sentenced to death.

In June 1965 the *Orlando Evening Star* carried a story announcing that 27,258 acres of land had been acquired by a certain Walt Disney and his brother Roy in preparation for Disney's second and larger theme park, Walt Disney World. Walt died in 1966, but his brother Roy continued his work, opening Walt Disney World to kids of all ages in 1971.

Closer to home, in an attempt to deal with escalating violence, the Northern Ireland Government introduced internment without trial to remove from the streets those it believed were responsible for violence. In a dawn raid on Monday 9 August, 3,000 soldiers backed by RUC special branch officers using out-of-date intelligence arrested 342 men. The majority of prisoners were held in a disused airfield at Long Kesh, which became HM Maze prison.

This was also a time of great technological advancement. Intel released the first microprocessor in 1971, and Philips launched the first VCR video recorder for home use.

But most of all I remember 1971 for the music, in particular The Doors, Santana, Black Sabbath, Deep Purple, Rod Stewart and the Faces, and above all Camel, whom I first saw in concert with Wishbone Ash in December 1971.

Enjoy the nostalgia!

Scotland

PERTH

Leaving Perth bus station on 31 May 1971 for the 15-mile journey north to Dunkeld is Midland MRD 170 (TWG 549), an ECW-bodied Bristol FLF6G new in May 1962; it would be sold for scrap in June 1979. *Author's collection*

The birth of Bangladesh is declared by the government in exile in territory formerly part of Pakistan.

Photo	DESTINATIONS
1	**SHEFFIELD** (Title page)
	SCOTLAND
2	**PERTH** (Previous page)
3	**ANNAN**
4	**EDINBURGH**
5	**EDINBURGH**
	TEESSIDE
6	**TEESSIDE**
	ISLE OF MAN
7	**DOUGLAS**
	LANCASHIRE & MERSEYSIDE
8	**BLACKPOOL**
9	**BLACKPOOL**
10	**BLACKPOOL**
11	**BLACKPOOL**
12	**BLACKPOOL**
13	**BLACKPOOL**

ANNAN Working service 80 to Dumfries on 24 September is Western SMT No DT1704 (TCS 152), one of 52 Bristol MW6Gs purchased new by Western SMT with Alexander coach bodywork; No 1704 was new in 1962. All the Bristol MWs remained in service until 1977, which would indicate excellent build quality and, at the time, excellent maintenance by Western SMT. *Author's collection*

On this day Britain expelled 90 KGB and GRU (Main Intelligence Directorate) officials, and 15 were not allowed to return.

Right: **EDINBURGH** The Mound was formed between 1781 and 1830 from an incredible 1½ million tons of earth and rubble left over from the construction of the New Town. Its inception followed the 1765 drainage of the old Nor' Loch, the stagnant basin of water that would one day become Princes Street Gardens. On The Mound on service 23 to Morningside on 1 October is No 497 (LFS 497), an MCCW-bodied Leyland PD2/20 new in November 1954; the bus was sold for scrap in April 1975, a month before Edinburgh Corporation became Lothian Regional Transport. *Author's collection*

On this day, Walt Disney World opened in Orlando, Florida.

EDINBURGH In Princes Street on 29 January, with the Scott Monument in the background, is No 708 (NSF 708), another MCCW-bodied Leyland PD2/20; this example was new in March 1956, and passed to Lothian Regional Transport in May 1975. The car on the left is a 1967 Renault 10 round-headlight version. *Author's collection*

On this day Clare Balding, broadcaster, journalist and author, was born in Hampshire.

Teesside

Isle of Man

TEESSIDE Between February and March 1970 Teesside Municipal Transport purchased eight all-Leyland PD2/1s from Leicester City Transport, where they had been that city's Nos 145 to 148, 153, and 157 to 159. This is Teesside No 147 (FJF 187) on 7 March 1971; it had been new in October 1950 and remained in the Teesside fleet until sold for scrap in April 1972. *Peter Taplin, Omnibus Society collection*

On this day the British postal workers' strike, led by Tom Jackson, ended after 47 days.

DOUGLAS The Douglas war memorial on Harris Promenade, seen in the middle background, was designed by Ewart Crellin and erected in May 1924. In front of the memorial on 31 August 1971 is Douglas Corporation No 68 (KMN 839), a Northern Counties-bodied AEC Regent II new in 1949; it later passed to Isle of Man Transport, but was never used. Note the horse tram on the left – the first horse cars ran on 7 August 1876. *Author's collection*

On this day golfer Padraig Harrington was born in Dublin.

lancashire and Merseyside

BLACKPOOL Standing in Rigby Road depot on 20 June is Bradford No 507 (NAK 507H), a Marshall-bodied AEC Swift new in September 1969. At the time this view was taken Blackpool also had a fleet of 16 of these vehicles, and another 40 were to arrive by August 1974. Standing alongside is Blackpool No 348 (PFR 348), an MCCW-bodied Leyland PD2/27 new in April 1959; it was purchased by R. I. Davies of Tredegar in February 1973 and remained with that fleet until June 1974. *Bob Gell*

The day after this picture was taken Britain began new negotiations for EEC membership in Luxembourg.

BLACKPOOL Standing in Blackpool bus station on the same day are North Western Road Car No 235 (JDB 235E) (left) and No 265 (KJA 265F), both Alexander-bodied Leyland PSU3/4Rs new in 1967 and 1968 respectively. *Bob Gell*

Eight days earlier Blackpool Football Club had won their first, and to date only, international trophy, beating Bologna in the Anglo-Italian Cup.

BLACKPOOL Also photographed in the bus station in Talbot Road on that same June day is Trent No 11 (PRC 211F), a Plaxton-bodied Leyland PSU3/4RT new in December 1967. *Bob Gell*

Six days earlier, on 14 June, Norway began oil production from the North Sea.

BLACKPOOL Between January 1934 and October 1934 12 open-top double-deck EEC trams, Nos 238 to 249, entered service and were known as 'Luxury Dreadnoughts'. Between August 1941 and June 1942 they were fitted with top covers by Blackpool Corporation and became known as 'Balloons'. Originally No 244, this is No 707 on 19 September 1971. *Author's collection*

On this day the electric tram system in the city of Ballarat, Victoria, Australia, closed.

Right: **BLACKPOOL** On the sea front on a wet 13 October is 'Balloon' No 722 (originally numbered 259 when new in January 1935). *Author's collection*

On this day the actor Sacha Baron Cohen was born in Hammersmith, London; he became well-known as the character Ali G, and provided the voice for King Julien XIII in the Madagascar movies.

BLACKPOOL A total of 18 'Coronation' cars, Nos 311 to 328, were delivered between January 1953 and January 1954; they had Roberts bodywork and were originally fitted with VAMBAC control equipment made by Allen West on behalf of Crompton Parkinson. One, No 313, was withdrawn in 1963, and the remainder were renumbered 648 to 664 in May 1968. This is No 655 on 18 September; it would be scrapped at Rigby Road depot in September 1976. *Author's collection*

On this day cyclist Lance Armstrong was born in Texas.

Photo	**DESTINATIONS**
	LANCASHIRE & MERSEYSIDE *Continued*
14	PRESTON
15	LEYLAND
16	ROSSENDALE
17	MANCHESTER
18	MANCHESTER
19	LEIGH
20	STOCKPORT
21	LIVERPOOL
22	LIVERPOOL
	YORKSHIRE
23	BRADFORD
24	DEWSBURY
25	DONCASTER
26	DONCASTER
27	DONCASTER
28	SHEFFIELD
29	SHEFFIELD
30	SHEFFIELD
31	SHEFFIELD
32	SHEFFIELD
33	SHEFFIELD

PRESTON bus station was officially opened on 12 October 1969, and leaving on 25 June 1971 is Preston No 15 (PRN 907), a Leyland Titan PD3/4 with MCW 'Orion' bodywork; the second of a batch of seven, it was new in October 1961. Preston eventually had 34 PD3s, 26 bought new with similar MCW bodywork, delivered between 1958 and 1965, and eight unique rebuilds from earlier Leyland-bodied PD2s. *Author's collection*

On this day Neil Lennon, the current Bolton FC manager, was born in Lurgan, Northern Ireland.

Right: **LEYLAND** W. H. Fowler was a commercial bodybuilder in Leyland, and built a few PSV bodies in the 1930s. In 1962 the company was purchased by J. W. Fishwick & Sons and from then on was run as the company's in-house body manufacturer. Fishwick built ten Fowler bus bodies, including three Leyland PSU4 Leopards (BTD 778J to 780J), which entered service in 1970. At Fishwick's depot on 19 June 1971 is the first of them. *Bob Gell*

The No 1 single on this day was Knock Three Times *by Dawn, and No 2 was* Middle of the Road *with* Chirpy Chirpy Cheep Cheep *(some of you will no doubt be singing along to these two now!).*

Left: **ROSSENDALE** On 12 August we see Rossendale No 23 (RTE 537), an East Lancashire-bodied Leyland PD2/12. New in 1953, it was originally No 23 in the Rawtenstall Corporation fleet, and retained its fleet number when the Rawtenstall and Haslingden fleets were merged in April 1968. Immediately behind is Greater Manchester PTE No 6310 (REN 610), an MCCW-bodied Leyland PDR1/1 new to Bury in 1963. *Author's collection*

On this day tennis player Pete Sampras was born in Potomac, Maryland.

MANCHESTER Nearest the camera in Piccadilly on 28 October is No 3052 (ARJ 203B) of SELNEC (the South East Lancashire North East Cheshire PTE); this MCCW-bodied Leyland PD2/40 was new to Salford Corporation in 1964. Working service 95 in the background is No 3454 (PND 454), an MCCW-bodied Leyland PD2/12 that was new to Manchester Corporation in 1956. *Bob Gell*

On this day the House of Commons voted 356 to 244 in favour of joining the European Economic Community.

MANCHESTER Still wearing Manchester Corporation livery on 14 July 1971 is SELNEC No 4441 (NNB 251), an MCCW-bodied Daimler CVG6K. *Author's collection*

Born on this day in Rotherham was the referee Howard Webb.

Scottish Omnibuses. A total of 252 Renowns were built. Standing in Leigh bus station on 28 October is SELNEC No 6928 (1975 TJ), one of the rear-entrance East Lancashire-bodied examples purchased in 1963. This bus still survives with the Yorkshire Heritage bus company. *Bob Gell*

While the House of Commons was debating EEC entry, on this day the UK became the sixth nation to launch a satellite into orbit.

Below: **STOCKPORT** Also photographed on 28 October, and still wearing the Stockport coat of arms two years after SELNEC was formed, are Nos 5876 (KJA 876F), an East Lancashire-bodied Leyland PD3/14 new in 1968, and 5817 (BJA 917B), a Leyland PD2/40 also bodies by East Lancashire and new in 1964. In the background is the Stockport railway viaduct, designed by George Watson Buck and completed in 1840. The 27-arch viaduct is 111 feet high, and 11 million bricks were used in its construction; at the peak of the work 600 labourers worked in shifts, night and day. *Bob Gell*

Eleven days after this view was taken Led Zeppelin released their fourth studio album, Led Zeppelin 4, which featured Stairway to Heaven; 23 million copies have been sold.

Above: **LEIGH** The AEC Renown was a bus chassis intended for low-height double-deck bodywork developed by AEC to replace the Bridgemaster. The model was introduced in the summer of 1962 and only the AV590 engine was offered; air suspension was used on the rear axle, while the front was a beam axle with leaf springs. The first production Renowns were bodied by Willowbrook and were purchased by South Wales Transport. Other customers were North Western and East Yorkshire, and municipal operators included Leicester, which ordered both front-entrance and rear-entrance examples; the only other rear-entrance bodies were ordered by Leigh Corporation. Nottingham and Wolverhampton Corporations added Renowns to their fleets, while eight chassis went to independents, one to

1971
No 1 Records

January

| Clive Dunn | *Grandad* |
| George Harrison | *My Sweet Lord* |

March

| Mungo Jerry | *Baby Jump* |
| T. Rex | *Hot Love* |

May

| Dave and Ansil Collins | *Double Barrel* |
| Dawn | *Knock Three Times* |

June

| Middle of the Road | *Chirpy Chirpy Cheep Cheep* |

July

| T. Rex | *Get It On* |

August

| Diana Ross | *I'm Still Waiting* |

September

| Tams | *Hey Girl Don't Bother Me* |

October

| Rod Stewart | *Maggie May* |

November

| Slade | *Coz I Luv You* |

December

| Benny Hill | *Ernie (The Fastest Milkman in the West)* |

Above: **LIVERPOOL** In March 1963 Liverpool Corporation took delivery of No L559 (559 KD), an MCCW-bodied Leyland PDR1 Mark II; it originally had a Leyland 0.600 engine, then was fitted with a Leyland 0.680 engine in January 1968 and re-seated for one person operation in October 1969. In December of that year L559 was transferred to Merseyside Passenger Transport Executive and is seen here still wearing the Liverpool coat of arms on 19 June 1971. *Bob Gell*

Yorkshire

Below: **BRADFORD** Between May and December 1945 Bradford Corporation took delivery of 17 Karrier Ws; Nos 703 to 714 had Roe bodywork, while 715 to 719 had bodies by Park Royal. On 24 April 1971 this is No 704 (DKY 704), which had its Roe body replaced by a new East Lancashire one in October 1959. The vehicle was purchased for preservation by the National Trolleybus Association in March 1973. *Author's collection*

On this day a tsunami 85 metres high rose over the Ryukyu Islands in Japan and deposited a 750-ton block of coral 2.5 kilometres inland!

Above: **LIVERPOOL** Leyland's L280 to L309 (VKB 736 to 765) were delivered to Liverpool Corporation in 1957 with Crossley frames to be completed by the Corporation. They were stored at Edge Lane until 1961 and the bodywork was completed by MCCW. Of this batch, Nos L294, L295, L300 and L303 to L309 were unpainted. On the same day as the previous view we see No L294 (VKB 750), which entered service in October 1961, working service 60 to Huyton. On the right is No A151 (SKB 151), a Crossley-bodied AEC Regent V new in June 1956, while in the background is 1128 (UKA 128H), an Alexander-bodied Leyland PDR2/1 new in 1970. *Bob Gell*

Right: **DEWSBURY** In 1964 Sheffield Joint Omnibus took delivery of No 1144 (350 HWE), a Park Royal-bodied AEC Regent V. It passed to Hebble Motor Services in February 1970, then on 1 April 1971 Hebble was acquired by Yorkshire Woollen, and the bus received fleet number 144, as seen here in Dewsbury bus station on 3 September. The bus passed to the Kowloon Omnibus Company of Hong Kong in September 1973. *Peter Taplin, Omnibus Society collection*

On this day Qatar gained independence from the United Kingdom.

Below: **DONCASTER** This is Doncaster Corporation No 147 (TDT 347), an exposed-radiator AEC Regent V with Roe bodywork new in 1956; the AEC code for this bus was MD3RV, which meant that it had the smaller six-cylinder 7.68-litre engine, a four-speed synchromesh gearbox and triple servo vacuum brakes. A passenger makes a dodgy exit on 17 June! *Author's collection*

On this day representatives of Japan and the USA signed the Okinawa Reversion Agreement whereby the USA returned control of Okinawa to Japan.

Below right: **DONCASTER** Photographed on 20 February, this is 891 GWT of Blue Line (Samuel Morgan Ltd), a Roe-bodied Guy Arab V new in 1963. Blue Line was sold to South Yorkshire Passenger Transport Executive (SYPTE) in March 1979, and this bus was withdrawn in June of that year, still licensed to Blue Line. *Author's collection*

On the day this view was taken in quiet South Yorkshire suburbia, 20 February 1971, 50 tornadoes raged through Mississippi, killing 74 people.

DONCASTER Caught by the camera in East Laith Gate on 27 May is Felix Motors No 43 (932 BWR), a Roe-bodied AEC Regent V new in 1962. *Author's collection*

Actor Paul Bettany was born in Shepherds Bush, London, on this day; his first big Hollywood role was A Knight's Tale *in 2001 – an excellent film.*

SHEFFIELD Working service 75 between Bradway, City and Sheffield Lane Top on a snowy 3 January 1971 is Sheffield Transport No 887 (887 WJ), a Weymann-bodied Leyland PDR1/1 new in October 1959. *Author's collection*

On this day the BBC Open University TV broadcasts began.

SHEFFIELD Transport ordered 71 AEC Regent Vs of the 2D3RA model and they were all delivered in 1960. No 1339 (6339 WJ), seen here on 3 July working service 75 to Bradway, was one of a batch of 25 with Roe bodywork that had platform doors manually operated by the conductor. Many of this batch were withdrawn in 1972, but a few were still in service in 1973. *Author's collection*

This was the day that Jim Morrison of The Doors was found dead in his bathtub in Paris, a sad day indeed for many, including myself, who very much appreciated the group's music.

Right: **SHEFFIELD** I think too many passengers have taken seats on the same side in this 4 December view of Sheffield No 1292 (YWB 292), a Roe-bodied Leyland PD2/20 new in 1957! *Author's collection*

On this day a Montreux casino burned down during a Frank Zappa concert, an event marked by the classic song Smoke on the Water by Deep Purple. The casino was rebuilt in 1975.

Below: **SHEFFIELD** Working service 46 to the City on 3 May is No 1293 (YWB 293), a Roe-bodied Leyland PD2/20 new in 1957. *Author's collection*

On this day Arsenal won the League Division 1 title at the home of their close rivals Tottenham Hotspur, with Ray Kennedy scoring the winner.

Right: **SHEFFIELD** Working service 17 on Christmas Eve 1971 is Sheffield No 1371, a Park Royal-bodied AEC Regent V new in 1964. *Author's collection*

On this day Enrique Martin Morales was born in San Juan, Puerto Rico, later better known to many as Ricky Martin (are you singing Livin' la Vida Loca…?)

SHEFFIELD On 18 February, working the joint service 69 between Rotherham and Sheffield, is Sheffield No 717 (RWJ 717), a Metro-Cammell Weymann-bodied Leyland PD2/12 new in 1954. In the background is the Odeon cinema in Corporation Street, which opened as the Regal in 1934. The rear end of the bus on the left is that of Rotherham No 145 (2145 ET), a Roe-bodied Daimler CVG6/30 new in July 1962. *Author's collection*

Danish golfer Thomas Bjorn was born in Silkeborg in Denmark on this day.

Photo	DESTINATIONS
	STAFFORDSHIRE
34	NEWCASTLE-UNDER-LYME
35	LONGTON
36	HANLEY
	DERBYSHIRE
37	CHESTERFIELD
38	SPONDON
	NOTTINGHAMSHIRE
39	NOTTINGHAM
40	NOTTINGHAM
41	NOTTINGHAM
42	NOTTINGHAM
	LEICESTERSHIRE
43	LEICESTER
44	LEICESTER

Staffordshire

Above right: **NEWCASTLE-UNDER-LYME** The date is 28 April 1971, and on the right is Potteries Motor Traction No SN1117 (TVT 117G), a Marshall-bodied Leyland PSU4A/4R new in November 1968; this bus was sold to a dealer in October 1980. In the centre is No H6656 (XVT 656), an MCCW-bodied Daimler CVG5 that was new in September 1956 and was later fitted with a Gardner 6LW engine before being withdrawn and sold in October 1971. Finally No H710 (710 AEH) was one of a batch of 15 MCCW-bodied Leyland PD3/4s that was delivered to PMT between August and September 1957; this vehicle was purchased by Berresford's of Cheddleton in May 1973, where it remained until December 1974. *Bob Gell*

The No 1 album on this day was Pearl by Janis Joplin, who had died on 4 October 1970 leaving enough recorded material to make an LP.

Right: **LONGTON** Potteries Motor Traction had the largest fleet of Daimler Roadliners in the world. The Plaxton-bodied timber framed bodies could have gone on to near normal service lives if they had been re-engined with Perkins V8s. However, the Marshall-bodied Roadliners were a disaster, and by 1972 the Metalastik toggle suspension units were failing – they were expensive to buy and a nightmare to replace. This is No S1055 (KVT 155E), a Plaxton-bodied Daimler SRC6 new in February 1967 and photographed on 28 April 1971; it was sold to a scrap dealer in December 1974. *Bob Gell*

The No 1 album this week was Motown Chartbusters Volume 5, which contained classics like War by Edwin Starr, Ain't No Mountain High Enough by Diana Ross and Tears of a Clown by Smokey Robinson and the Miracles.

Derbyshire

CHESTERFIELD Delivered to Chesterfield Corporation in December 1963 were ten Weymann-bodied Daimler CCG6s, Nos 251 to 260 (3251 to 3260 NU). On service 51 to Hasland on 24 February 1971 is No 255 (3255 NU), which became a driver trainer in October 1972 until August 1976, when it was damaged in an accident and sold to a dealer. In the background is No 19 (496 ALH), one of three Willowbrook-bodied AEC Reliances acquired in November 1973 from London Transport; it was sold to the London Bus Preservation Group, Cobham, in April 1978. *Bob Gell*

Born the following day was actor Sean Astin, best known for his role as Samwise Gamgee in the Lord of the Rings films.

HANLEY During 1959 Yorkshire Woollen District took delivery of 15 MCCW-bodied AEC Regent Vs, Nos 796 to 810 (DHD 176 to 190). All had a relatively short service life with that operator, and the first to go (DHD 184 to 190) passed to Hebble in early 1970. DHD 184 was sold on to a dealer in August 1970 and was purchased by Stonier's of Goldenhill in January the following year, and is seen here leaving Hanley bus station on 28 April. *Bob Gell*

Born on this day was actress Bridget Moynahan, best known for her roles in I, Robot and The Sum of all Fears.

SPONDON This lovely view of Trent No 765 (KCH 108), an MCCW-bodied Leyland PD2/12 new in 1957, was taken Sancroft Road, Spondon, Derby, on 5 July. Note the advertisement for Nottingham Festival 71, taking place between 10 and 25 July at the Albert Hall in Nottingham. *Peter Taplin, Omnibus Society collection*

On 9 July at Nottingham's Albert Hall, Uriah Heep were supported by Sha-na-na.

Nottingham and Leicester

NOTTINGHAM Barton Transport Limited acquired a large number of Leyland 7RTs from London Transport; ten arrived between March and December 1967, and representing this batch 4 February 1971 is No 1084 (KYY 731), an MCCW-bodied Leyland 7RT new in May 1950. It remained with Barton until February 1973, when it was sold to the Royal Army Veterinary Corps in Melton Mowbray. *Author's collection*

On the day this view was taken, Rolls Royce became bankrupt and was nationalised.

NOTTINGHAM No 248 (XTO 248) was one of a large batch of Park Royal-bodied AEC Regent Vs delivered during 1956; this particular example was new in October of that year. It is seen on Victoria Embankment, Nottingham, on the former trolleybus route 45 on 25 February 1971; in December 1975 it was sold to George's Coaches, Coventry, where it remained until April 1978. *Bob Gell*

The album Jesus Christ Superstar was No 1 this week, and I was totally unaware that Ian Gillan of Deep Purple was the lead vocalist on it.

NOTTINGHAM At Huntingdon Street bus station on 7 August is MRR 974, an all-Leyland PSU1/13 new to South Notts in March 1952; it was withdrawn from the fleet seven months after this picture was taken. In the background is MVD 627, a Northern Counties-bodied Leyland PD2/12 new to Irvine of Salsburgh in 1956 and acquired by South Notts in November 1960; this bus would be exported to the USA in January 1974. *Bob Gell*

On 26 July 1971 Apollo 15 was successfully launched and returned safely to earth on the day this view was taken.

NOTTINGHAM In January 1971 Nottingham took delivery of six NCME-bodied Leyland PDR1/3s, Nos 395 to 400 (VAU 395J to 400J). They were 30ft 6in long by 8ft 2½in wide, and were built to a low height of 13ft 8in to pass under a low bridge in Wilford Lane (which was removed in September 1974). This is the first of the six, working service 67 on 25 July. After only ten years in the Nottingham fleet, all six were sold to a dealer in January 1981, and five were exported to Hong Kong in May of that year. *Bob Gell*

The No 1 album on this day was Carole King's Tapestry, *containing two much-liked songs,* I Feel the Earth Move *and* You've got a Friend.

LEICESTER Standing in Abbey Road depot on 16 May is No 183 (UJF 183), one of a batch of five MCCW-bodied Daimler CSG6-30s that were new in July and August 1959. Very soon after this view was taken all five passed to OK Motor Service Ltd of Bishop Auckland, but only two entered service with that operator (Nos 179 and 184). No 183 was later noted with D. Grierson Ltd, Fishburn, and was sold for scrap in December 1976. Alongside it is No 139 (WBC 139J), an MCW/Scania BR111MH that was brand new when this photograph was taken. *Bob Gell*

LEICESTER New to Leicester City Transport as No 44 (FJF 44D), this bus was one of a batch of ten rear-entrance AEC Renowns built to normal height dimensions on a low-height chassis, with a seating capacity of 74. Due to passenger complaints when they entered service, they were returned to the body builders, East Lancashire of Blackburn, for modifications to the lower saloon floor and rear platform. No 44 had a short working life, being sold to a dealer in January 1976 and scrapped in September 1977. This view was taken on 29 February 1971. *Bob Gell*

On this day Jari Litmanen, who played football for Ajax and Liverpool, among many others, was born in Lahti, Finland.

Photo	DESTINATIONS
WALSALL & BIRMINGHAM	
45	WALSALL
46	WALSALL
47	BIRMINGHAM
	EAST MIDLANDS
48	STAMFORD
49	PETERBOROUGH
	OXFORD, CHELTENHAM & BRISTOL
50	OXFORD
51	OXFORD
52	OXFORD
53	CHELTENHAM
54	CHELTENHAM
55	CHELTENHAM
56	BRISTOL

Walsall and Birmingham

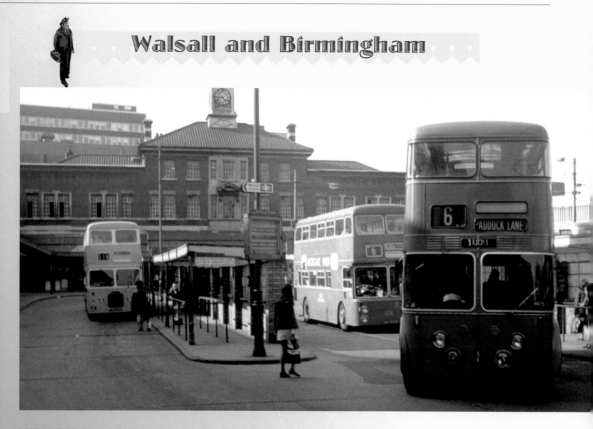

This picture was taken the day before actor Ewan McGregor was born in Perth, Scotland.

WALSALL Seen at Walsall bus station on 30 March 1971 is the unique No 1 (1 UDH), a Northern Counties-bodied Daimler CRG6LX new in November 1962. It had been exhibited at the 1962 Commercial Motor Show and featured a shortened wheelbase and reduced overhang to give an overall length of 25ft 7½in. By contrast, behind it is the more traditional Northern Counties-bodied Daimler CRG6LX No 106 (XDH 196G). On the left is another unique bus, No 56 (XDH 56G), a Northern Counties-bodied Daimler CRC6-36; this had been exhibited at the 1968 Commercial Motor Show; was fitted with a Cummins V6-200 engine and, when this view was taken, had seating for 85. No 1 was unfortunately scrapped in June 1977, but 56 is in preservation at the Birmingham & Midland Motor Omnibus Trust at Wythall. *Bob Gell*

1971 Happenings (1)

January

A stairway crush at a Rangers v Celtic football match at Ibrox kills 66

The Aswan High Dam officially opens in Egypt

Representatives of 23 western oil companies begin negotiations with OPEC in Tehran to stabilise oil prices

In Uganda, Idi Amin deposes Milton Obote in a coup to become president

In Los Angeles Charles Manson and three of his female 'family' members are found guilty of the 1969 Tate-LaBianca murders

Apollo 14 lifts off on the 31st and lands on the moon on 5 February, returning to earth on the 9th

February

Rolls Royce becomes bankrupt and is nationalised

The UK, US, USSR and others sign the Seabed Treaty, outlawing nuclear weapons on the ocean floor

In the Vietnam War, South Vietnamese troops invade Laos, backed by American air and artillery support

On the 15th the UK and Ireland both switch to decimal currency

Evel Knievel sets a world record and jumps 19 cars in Ontario, California

March

A British postal workers' strike ends after 47 days

In the 'Fight of the Century' boxer Joe Frazier defeats Muhammad Ali at Madison Square Garden

In the US *The Ed Sullivan Show* is broadcast for the last time

WALSALL Note the trolleybus wiring in this view of the bus station taken on the same day. The bus is West Midlands Passenger Transport Executive (WMPTE) No 2649 (JOJ 649), an MCCW-bodied Daimler CVD6 new to Birmingham Corporation in 1951; it would be one of a number of Birmingham buses to remain in service past their sell-by dates to replace Walsall trolleybuses. *Bob Gell*

The hit songs on this day were Hot Love *by T. Rex,* Rose Garden *by Lynn Anderson,* Power to the People *by John Lennon and Yoko Ono,* Strange Kind of Woman *by Deep Purple,* Sweet Caroline *by Neil Diamond,* My Sweet Lord *by George Harrison,* My Way *by Frank Sinatra, and* Grandad *by Clive Dunn.*

BIRMINGHAM This is WMPTE No 3205 (MOF 205), a Crossley-bodied Daimler CVG6 that was new in 1953 but entered service in 1954; it is working service 6 to Bearwood on 9 May. *Author's collection*

On this day Arsenal beat Liverpool 2-1 to win the English FA Cup, thus completing the League and Cup double.

East Midlands

STAMFORD In October 1954 United Counties took delivery of four ECW-bodied Bristol LS6Bs, Nos 490 to 493 (JBD 995 to 998), and No 492 is seen here in Stamford bus station on 12 June; six months later it was sold to a dealer for scrap. *Bob Gell*

1971 Happenings (2)

PETERBOROUGH Between February and July 1967 United Counties took delivery of its last Bristol FLFs, Nos 719 to 738. Picking up passengers at Peterborough bus station for a service to Kettering on 12 June 1971 is No 725 (KNV 725E), a Bristol FLF6B that was new in February 1967 and withdrawn from service in 1980. *Bob Gell*

April
Mount Etna erupts in Sicily
The People's Republic of Bangladesh is formed, but the government flees to India
Sierra Leone becomes a republic
The Soviet Union launches Salyut 1, which later docks with Soyuz 10
François Duvalier ('Papa Doc'), President of Haiti, dies and is succeeded as President-for-life by his son Jean-Claude Duvalier ('Baby Doc')
500,000 people in Washington DC and 125,000 in San Francisco march in protest against the Vietnam War

May
Amtrak begins inter-city rail passenger services in the United States
The Harris Poll claims that 60% of Americans oppose the Vietnam War
An air crash at Rijeka Airport, Yugoslavia, kills 78 people, mostly British tourists
US launches Mariner 9 toward Mars
The birth of Bangladesh, in territory formerly part of Pakistan, is declared by the government in exile

June
Vietnam Veterans for a Just Peace, claiming to represent the majority of US veterans who served in South-East Asia, speak against Vietnam War protests
Concert promoter Bill Graham closes the legendary Fillmore East in New York City, which had opened on 8 March 1968
After a successful mission aboard Salyut 1, the world's first manned space station, the crew of the Soyuz 11 die when their air supply leaks out through a faulty valve

Oxford, Cheltenham and Bristol

OXFORD Stratford Blue purchased two Plaxton Panorama-bodied Leyland L2Ts in May 1964, and this is one of them. Originally numbered 57 in the Stratford Blue fleet, the bus passed with that company's business to Midland Red on 1 January 1971, and is seen here as No 2057 (AAC 22B) en route to Coventry from Gloucester Green, Oxford, on 15 August. It was withdrawn from service in January 1976.
Bob Gell

On this day the number of British troops in Northern Ireland was raised to 12,500.

OXFORD On the same day in Gloucester Green, en route to Portsmouth, is Royal Blue
No 2280 (768 MDV), an ECW-bodied Bristol MW6G new in 1963. In August 1976 this
bus was noted with Press International. *Bob Gell*

OXFORD During 1962 Aldershot & District took delivery of a batch of dual-purpose Park Royal-bodied AEC Reliances. City of Oxford acquired a number of these in 1970, and seen in Gloucester Green in the livery of Oxford/South Midland is No 70 (426 DHO). I was living in Banbury when this view was taken on 15 August. *Bob Gell*

A few months before this date I managed to acquire a ticket for the Yes Album Tour, which visited Oxford on 7 May 1971.

CHELTENHAM
The next three views were all taken at Cheltenham coach station on 3 July 1971. Nearing the end of its coach service life is Red & White No 958 (SWO 988), an ECW coach-bodied Bristol MW6G new in 1958. *Bob Gell*

On this day John Newcombe from Australia beat Stan Smith from the USA to win the Wimbledon Men's Singles final.

Right: **CHELTENHAM** East Kent took delivery of four 53-seat Plaxton coach-bodied AEC Reliances in May 1971, and representing this batch is WJG 472J. *Bob Gell*

The No 1 single on this day in the USA was It's Too Late/I Feel The Earth Move by Carole King.

CHELTENHAM Even in the early 1970s Cheltenham coach station was renowned for hundreds of coaches heading in all directions. Wallace Arnold, Yorkshire Traction and Yorkshire Woollen coaches would stop for refreshment breaks en route from Yorkshire to Devon and vice versa. This is Yorkshire Traction No 234 (YHE 234J), the first of four Alexander-bodied Leyland PSU3B/4Rs new in May 1971. *Bob Gell*

BRISTOL A total of 218 examples of the Bristol FSF were constructed and delivered to 11 operators between 1960 and 1963. Bristol took delivery of 34 between October 1960 and October 1961, and representing the batch is No 6010 (709 JHY), photographed in Bristol city centre on 5 July. This bus passed to Wiltshire Area Health Authority, Odstock Hospital, Salisbury, in October 1976, and was sold at auction in March 1979. *Bob Gell*

On this day the 26th Amendment to the United States Constitution was certified by Richard Nixon, lowering the voting age from 21 to 18.

1971 Happenings (3)

July

The first 'e-book', a copy of the US Declaration of Independence, is posted on the mainframe computer at the University of Illinois

President Richard Nixon announces that he will visit China in 1972

The South Tower of the World Trade Center is topped out; at 415 metres (1,362 feet) it is the world's second tallest building

Apollo 15 is launched, and two crew members become the first to ride in a lunar rover the day after landing on the moon

The UK opts out of the 'space race' with the cancellation of its 'Black Arrow' launch vehicle

August

Apollo 15 returns to earth

British security forces arrest hundreds of Irish nationalists and intern them without trial in Long Kesh prison; 20 people die in the riots that follow. Troops are stationed on the border to stop arms smuggling

Bahrain declares independence

Jackie Stewart becomes Formula 1 World Driver's Champion in his Tyrrell-Cosworth

Photo DESTINATIONS

WALES
57 WEST MONMOUTHSHIRE
LONDON
58 KINGSTON-UPON-THAMES
59 UXBRIDGE
60 LONDON
61 VICTORIA COACH STATION
62 VICTORIA COACH STATION
THE SOUTH COAST
63 EASTBOURNE
64 SOUTHAMPTON
65 WEYMOUTH
THE SOUTH WEST
66 EXETER
67 EXETER
68 PAIGNTON
69 PLYMOUTH
70 PLYMOUTH (Front cover)

Wales

WEST MONMOUTHSHIRE This is West Monmouthshire Omnibus Board No 10 (FCH 19), a Saro-bodied Leyland PSUC1/1 that had been new to Trent in November 1954; it was purchased from Davies of Tredegar in December 1968 and sold on to Way of Cardiff Docks a short time after this view was taken on 17 May 1971. *Peter Taplin, Omnibus Society collection*

On this day Vernett Bennett was born in London, best known as a founding member of the girl group Eternal.

London

KINGSTON UPON THAMES Working from Fulwell depot on service 71 on 20 January 1971 is No RT579 (HLX 396). New in July 1948, at the time of this view it was fitted with a Weymann body. The last depot to which it was allocated was Catford in February 1978, and four months later it was sold for scrap. *Author's collection*

On this day Gary Barlow of Take That was born.

UXBRIDGE This is London Transport No RF 391 (MXX 279), a Metro-Cammell-bodied AEC Regal IV new in January 1953, working route 223 from Uxbridge depot on 21 October. Behind, working route 140 out of Harrow Weald depot, is No RT2655 (LYR 639), a Park Royal-bodied AEC Regent III new in August 1951. *Author's collection*

On this day 22 people lost their lives in a gas explosion at a shopping centre in Clarkston, Renfrewshire.

VICTORIA COACH STATION Working the Yeovil/Exeter-London coach service on 14 June 1971 is Western National No W1464 (OTA 636G), an ECW-bodied Bristol RELH6G new in 1969. *Bob Gell*

On this day the first Hard Rock Café opened in Piccadilly, London.

VICTORIA COACH STATION When this
view was taken on Monday 13 September Black
& White No 327 (YDF 327K), a Plaxton-bodied
Leyland PSU3B/4R, had been in service for less
than a month. *Bob Gell*

*The Baker Street bank heist was first reported
on this day. Thieves had tunnelled into the vault
of Lloyds Bank on Baker Street in London and
ransacked the safety deposit boxes, making off with
a haul estimated at the time to be in the region of
£500,000. In fact, the robbers looted in excess of
£3 million, which made it the largest British bank
robbery to date.*

South Coast

EASTBOURNE In July 1962 Eastbourne took delivery
of five East Lancashire-bodied AEC Regent Vs, Nos 61
to 65 (JJK 261 to 265). Delivered in blue and primrose
livery, they were repainted into cream with light blue lining
during 1968 and 1969. No 61, seen here on 10 June 1971,
would be the last to survive in the Eastbourne fleet, being
sold in February 1980. *Author's collection*

On this day the USA ended its trade embargo with China.

1971 Happenings (4)

September

Qatar gains independence from the UK, but declines to become part of either the United Arab Emirates or Saudi Arabia

The John F. Kennedy Center for the Performing Arts is inaugurated in Washington DC, opening with Leonard Bernstein's *Mass*

October

Walt Disney World opens in Orlando, Florida

Greenpeace is founded in Vancouver, Canada

The UN General Assembly admits the People's Republic of China but expels the Republic of China (Taiwan)

The Democratic Republic of Congo is renamed Zaire

The total number of US troops still in Vietnam drops to a record low of 196,700

In Northern Ireland Rev Ian Paisley established his Democratic Unionist Party

A bomb explodes at the top of the Post Office Tower in London

November

President Richard Nixon sets 1 February 1972 as the deadline for the removal of a further 45,000 American troops from Vietnam

Mariner 9 becomes the first spacecraft to successfully enter the orbit of Mars

SOUTHAMPTON During 1963 Southampton Corporation took delivery of ten Park Royal-bodied Leyland PD2A/27s and 15 East Lancashire-bodied AEC Regent Vs. The Leylands arrived first, in February, and the AECs were delivered in November. This picture, comparing AEC No 354 (left) and Leyland No 337, was taken on 24 November. *Author's collection*

On this day, during a severe storm over Washington State, a man calling himself D. B. Cooper parachuted from a Northwest Orient Airlines plane he had hijacked with $200,000 in ransom money and was never seen again. While FBI investigators have stated from the beginning that Cooper probably did not survive his risky jump, the agency maintains an active case file.

WEYMOUTH On 4 July we see Wilts & Dorset No 927 (PEL 906G), a Duple Northern-bodied Bedford VAL70. In later years this coach was owned by the Royals Jazz Band and was parked off Newcastle Street in Burslem, Stoke-on-Trent, then later in Baddeley Green on the side of the A53. By 1991 it had been converted to a transporter and was noted at an autograss race meeting at Lydstep in Pembrokeshire. *Bob Gell*

At No 4 in the charts on this day was a favourite of mine, Get it On by T. Rex.

 # The South West

Left: **EXETER** Seven Marshall-bodied Leyland PSUR1B/1Rs, Nos 211 to 217 (TDV 211J to 217J), were ordered by Exeter Corporation and delivered to Devon General in September 1970. This is No 212 (TDV 212J), still in Exeter Corporation livery on 9 August 1971 and now owned by Western National, which had acquired Devon General on 1 January. *Bob Gell*

The day after this picture was taken footballer Roy Keane was born in Cork, Ireland.

Lower left: **EXETER** Leaving the bus station on the same day is Greenslades 941 GTA. This AEC Reliance was new to Devon General in June 1961, with a Willowbrook body 7ft 6in wide, and was acquired by Greenslades in October 1970. *Bob Gell*

Around about this time in Swindon I was in a record store purchasing Rod Stewart's album Every Picture Tells a Story, *which in my opinion had two outstanding tracks,* Maggie May *and* Reason to Believe.

Left: **PAIGNTON** Working local service 108 in Paignton on 31 October is Western National No 1878 (RTT 997), an ECW-bodied Bristol LD6B that was new in 1954 and was exported to Amsterdam in September 1976. *Author's collection*

On this day a bomb, responsibility for which was claimed by the Provisional IRA, exploded in the roof of the men's toilets at the top of the Post Office Tower, London.

1971 Happenings (5)

November

Intel releases the world's first microprocessor, the Intel 4004

December

Pakistan launches pre-emptive attacks against nine Indian air bases, followed the next day by an invasion of East Pakistan by India

President Richard Nixon orders the US 7th Fleet to move towards the Bay of Bengal in the Indian Ocean

The Pakistan Army in East Pakistan (now Bangladesh) surrenders to the freedom fighters of Bangladesh, ending the Bangladesh Liberation War

Stanley Kubrick's controversial film *A Clockwork Orange* is released

The UK gives up its military bases in Malta

1971 Arrivals & Departures

Arrivals

Mary J. Blige	Singer	11 January
Kid Rock	Singer	17 January
Gary Barlow	Singer/songwriter	20 January
Clare Balding	Sports presenter	29 January
Patrick Kielty	Comedian and presenter	31 January
Damian Lewis	Actor	11 February
Amanda Holden	Actress	16 February
Sean Astin	Actor	25 February
John Hamm	Actor	10 March
David Coulthard	Racing driver	27 March
Ewan McGregor	Actor	31 March
Jacques Villeneuve	Racing driver	9 April
David Tennant	Actor	18 April
Sofia Coppola	Film director	14 May
Paul Bettany	Actor	27 May
Mark Wahlberg	Actor	5 June
Neil Lennon	Footballer	25 June
Missy 'Misdemeanor' Elliott	Singer/songwriter	1 July
Julian Assange	Australian activist	3 July
Alison Krauss	Singer	23 July
Roy Keane	Footballer	10 August
Pete Sampras	Tennis player	12 August
David Walliams	Comedy actor	20 August
Richard Armitage	Actor	22 August
Padraig Harrington	Golfer	31 August
David Arquette	Actor	8 September
Martin Freeman	Actor	8 September
Stella McCartney	Fashion designer	13 September
Amy Poehler	Actress	16 September
Lance Armstrong	Cyclist	18 September
Jada Pinkett Smith	Actress	18 September
Luke Wilson	Actor	21 September
Chesney Hawkes	Singer/songwriter	22 September
Jessie Wallace	Actress	25 September
Tiffany	Singer	2 October
Evgeny Kissin	Pianist	10 October
Sacha Baron Cohen	Comedian and actor	13 October
Andy Cole	Footballer	14 October
Snoop Dogg (Calvin Broadus)	Rapper	20 October
Dannii Minogue	Singer	20 October
Jade Jagger	Jewellery designer	2i October
Winona Ryder	Actress	29 October
Dylan Moran	Comedian and writer	3 November
Adam Gilchrist	Cricketer	14 November
Richard Krajicek	Tennis player	6 December
Arantxa Sanchez Vicario	Tennis player	18 December
Tara Palmer-Tompkinson	Socialite	23 December
Ricky Martin	Singer	24 December
Dido (Florian Cloud de Bounevialle Armstrong)	Singer	25 December

Departures

Coco Chanel	Fashion designer	(b1883)	10 January
Harold Lloyd	Silent film actor	(b1893)	8 March
Igor Stravinsky	Composer	(b1882)	6 April
Cecil Parker	Actor	(b1897)	20 April
'Papa Doc' Duvalier	President of Haiti	(b1907)	21 April
Sir Tyrone Guthrie	Director /producer/writer	(b1900)	15 May
Ogden Nash	Poet	(b1902)	19 May
Audie Murphy	War hero and actor	(b1924)	28 May
Michael Rennie	Actor	(b1909)	10 June
Ambrose	Bandleader	(b1896)	11 June
Lord (John) Reith	First Director-General of the BBC	(b1889)	16 June
Jim Morrison	Singer/songwriter	(b1943)	3 July
Louis Armstrong	Jazz musician	(b1901)	6 July
Van Heflin	Actor	(b1910)	23 July
Alan Rawsthorne	Composer	(b1905)	24 July
Paul Lukas	Actor	(b1895)	15 August
Nikita Khrushchev	Soviet leader	(b1894)	11 September
Gene Vincent	Singer	(b1935)	12 October
A. P. Herbert	Humorist, writer and law reform activist	(b1890)	11 November
Dame Gladys Cooper	Actress	(b1888)	17 November
Roy Disney	Film executive	(b1873)	20 December
Max Steiner	Film composer	(b1888)	28 December
Pete Duel	Actor (*Alias Smith and Jones*)	(b1940)	31 December

PLYMOUTH At Bretonside bus station in Plymouth on 6 August 1971 are, on the left, Royal Blue No 1434 (HDV 639E), an ECW-bodied Bristol MW6G, and No 2366 (HDV 625E), an ECW-bodied Bristol RELH6G, both new in 1967. No 1434 is currently preserved by Stagecoach and is reputed to be the first vehicle purchased by Gloagtrotter (Brian Soutar, Ann Gloag and her husband). *Bob Gell*

Six days later the film Willy Wonka and the Chocolate Factory *with Gene Wilder was released in the UK.*

Front cover: **PLYMOUTH** Between April and June 1958 Plymouth Corporation took delivery of 21 Metro-Cammell-bodied Leyland PD2/40s, and representing this batch on 6 July 1971 is No 112 (OCO 512), which remained in the Plymouth fleet until April 1974 and was sold to Eynon of Trimsaran two months later; Eynon sold it for scrap in September of the following year. *Author's collection*

On this day jazz trumpeter Louis Armstrong died in Queens, New York.

Back cover: **ILKESTON** At White Lion Square in Ilkeston on 5 July 1971 is Barton No 996 (996 VRR), a Harrington-bodied Bedford VAL14 new in May 1964. In August 1973 it passed to Prospect of Stourbridge, then to All Seasons Tours Limited, Eardington, in June 1976. By March 1978 No 996 had been rebuilt as a transporter. *Bob Gell*

On this day Derek McInnes, the current Aberdeen FC manager, was born in Paisley.

Index of operators and vehicles

Barton: KYY 731   26
Black & White: YDF 327K   44
Blackpool: NAK 507H, PFR 348   7; tram 707   9; trams 655, 722   10
Bradford: DKY 704   17
Bristol: 709 JHY   41

Chesterfield: 3255 NU   24

Doncaster: TDT 347, 891 GWT   18; 932 BWR   19
Douglas (IoM): KMN 839   6

East Kent: WJG 472J   40
Eastbourne: JJK 261   44
Edinburgh: LFS 497, NSF 708   5
Exeter: TDV 212J   46

Fishwick, J. & Sons: BTD 778J   12

Greenslades: 941 GTA   46

Leicester: UJF 183, WBC 193J   29; FJF 44D   30
Liverpool: 559 KD   16; VKB 750   17
London Transport: HLX 396   42; MXX 279   43

Manchester: PND 454   13
Midland (Scotland): TWG 549   3
Midland Red: AAC 22B   36

North Western Road Car: JDB 235E, KJA 265F   7
Nottingham: XTO 248   26; VAU 395J   28

Oxford: 426 DHO   38

Potteries Motor Traction: TVT 117G, XVT 656, KVT 155E   23
Preston: PRN 907   11

Red & White: SWO 988   39
Rossendale: RTE 537   12
Royal Blue: 768 MDV   37; HDV 639E, HDV 625E   48

SELNEC: ARJ 203B   13 ; NNB 251   14; 1975 TJ   15; KJA 876F, BJA 917B   15
Sheffield: VWE 73   1; 887 WJ   19; 6339 WJ   20; YWB 292, YWB 293, 371 HWE   21; RWJ 717   22
South Notts: MRR 974   27
Southampton: 374 FCR, 337 AOW   45
Stonier's: DHD 184   24

Teesside: FJF 187   6
Trent: PRC 211F   8; KCH 108   25

United Counties: JBD 997   34; KNV 725E   35

Walsall: 1 UDH, XDH 195G, XDH 56G   31
West Monmouthshire: FCH 19   42
Western National: OTA 636G   43; RTT 997   46
Western SMT: TCS 152   4
Wilts & Dorset: PEL 906G   45
WMPTE: JOJ 649   32; MOF 205   33

Yorkshire Traction: YHE 234J   40
Yorkshire Woollen: 350 HWE   18